Cycl

CW00336843

Cycles & Cycling

Martin Ayres

Newnes Technical Books

Newnes Technical Books

is an imprint of the Butterworth Group

which has principal offices in

London, Sydney, Toronto, Wellington, Durban and Boston

First published 1981

© Butterworth & Co (Publishers) Ltd, 1981

British Library Cataloguing in Publication Data

Ayres, Martin
   Cycles and cycling. – (Questions & answers).
   1. Bicycles
   I. Title   II. Series
   629.2'272   TL410

   ISBN 0-408-00484-3

Typeset by Butterworths Litho Preparation Department
Printed in England by Butler & Tanner Ltd, Frome and London

PREFACE

After many years in the doldrums cycling for leisure, or as a convenient means of transport, is enjoying a long overdue revival. The recovery began with the introduction of small-wheel machines in the early 1960s, and gathered momentum as people turned to the bicycle for exercise in the fitness-conscious seventies. More recently the ever-increasing cost of fuel has further boosted interest in cycling as the most economical form of transport.

Today the bicycle buyer is faced with a baffling variety of machines, ranging from small-wheel folding machines that pack away into the boot of a car, to 10-speed racing models equipped with all the latest expensive equipment.

Most people's requirements lie somewhere between these extremes, and this book will help the newcomer to cycling to choose the machine best suited to his or her needs. For those already converted to pedal power there is guidance on getting the best out of a bicycle with tips on maintenance and repairs.

M.A.

CONTENTS

1

BUYING A BICYCLE

What types of bicycle are available?

There are three main types: the traditional roadster, the small-wheel machine and the lightweight sports.

What are the main features of each type?

The *roadster* is built for comfort rather than speed. Its low mattress-type saddle and up-turned handlebars give a 'sit-up-and-beg' riding position, most of the components are made from steel, and it will usually have a hub three-speed gear, rod operated brakes and wide section wheels.

Small-wheel machines are unisex cycles which can be ridden by all the family, thanks to the wide range of saddle and handlebar adjustments that are possible.

Sports and racing models are light in weight, have dropped handlebars, cable-operated brakes, narrow section wheels and tyres, and five, ten or even twelve gears.

Fig. 1. Roadster

What points should a cycle buyer bear in mind?

Thought must be given to the purpose for which the cycle is to be used. Roadsters and small-wheel machines are ideal for shopping and other short journeys, but are not really practical for more than three miles (5 km). If more ambitious distances are planned, and certainly for touring, then a lightweight sports would be a better choice.

Fig. 2. Small-wheel bicycle

Fig. 3. Sports lightweight

Fig. 4. A successful folding bicycle

Fig. 5. The frame hinges for folding

What are the relative merits of the three types of machine?

The roadster is generally cheaper than the other models, and because it is solidly built should give reliable service for many years with a minimum of maintenance. A small-wheeler takes up less space in a shed or garage, is available in folding form for packing into a car, and because of its unique frame shape can carry large loads in safety on front and rear carriers. A sports machine will not stand up to too much rough treatment, but it is lighter, offers a wider range of gear ratios and gives a more efficient riding position.

How important is the weight of a cycle?

The lighter the cycle is the easier it will be to ride. A sports model weighing about 23 lb (10 kg) will obviously need less physical effort to pedal it along than a 45 lb (20 kg) roadster. The lighter machine will also be more responsive and maneouvrable. The difference is not so important on level roads, but a lightweight has a real advantage when climbing hills.

Why are sports models more expensive?

The main reasons are costlier materials and more elaborate accessories. The frame is made from high-grade steel tubing, components such as handlebars, chainwheels, rims and hubs are made from aluminium alloys rather than steel, and many components such as gears and alloy chainsets have to be imported.

Is it possible to buy an all-British bicycle?

There are probably a few roadster and small-wheel models of wholly British origin, but most models are a mixture of British and imported components. Some of the most popular British products are frame tubing, leather saddles and hub gears. One of the world's largest cycle manufacturing companies is Raleigh Industries, which employs more than 10 000 people at its Nottingham factories.

Where can I buy a bicycle?

There is a wide range of retail outlets – local bike shops, High Street multiples, department stores, garages, mail order catalogues. They all offer similar ranges of machines. But when buying don't let price be the only consideration. Shop around, and ask the retailer what facilities he can offer in the way of after-sales service and repairs.

Can a bicycle be insured?

Yes, dealers who are members of a national traders association will often arrange insurance on machines purchased from them.

Most insurance companies include coverage for bicycles in their household contents schemes, and several offer policies separate from household schemes. Members of the main cycling organisations, e.g. in the UK the Cyclists' Touring Club and British Cycling Federation, are also able to take advantage of insurance schemes which include third party cover.

Are new bicycles supplied ready for the road, or is it necessary to buy extras?

It should be possible to ride a new bicycle away from the shop, and an experienced dealer will check that it is roadworthy before handing it over. As a rule manufacturers do not include in their specifications 'extras' such as lamps, pumps, bells, toe-clips and straps, carrier and cycle bags.

How can a buyer choose the correct cycle size?

A specialist cycle dealer will be able to advise on the most suitable size. Care should be taken, for a cycle that does not fit can prove a costly mistake. One that is too small will be uncomfortable to ride, and if it is a child's cycle the child will quickly outgrow it. A cycle with a frame that is too large offers fewer alternative saddle and handlebar positions. It can also be dangerous if the rider is sitting too high.

One method of fitting the cycle to the rider is to stand astride the top tube. If the feet can just rest flat on the floor then the frame size is about right. If the rider can only stand on tip-toe, something smaller is called for, and if there is a gap between the crutch and top tube a larger frame is required.

What are the pitfalls in buying a secondhand machine?

Although a secondhand machine may have seen better days most components can be replaced fairly cheaply, so do not be put off by tyres that have been worn smooth, brake or gear cables in need of replacement, or missing spokes. But what cannot be repaired or replaced inexpensively is the frame. Look out for signs that it has been in a collision. The forks may be bent back, or the frame may be twisted: study it from the back to ensure that the wheels are in line. Most frequently overlooked are bent top and down tubes. Check for signs of cracked paintwork behind the top and bottom head lugs and run the fingers round the tubes at these points for tell-tale ripples. If any of these signs are present the bike probably is not worth bothering with.

Spin the wheels to check that the rims run true. Slight buckles can be rectified, but look out for rims with dents or flats; they will almost certainly need replacing, which with the cost of rebuilding the wheel can be an expensive job.

Check also that the gears work, particularly a hub gear, which can also be expensive to replace. It may be in need of adjustment, but it should work reasonably well.

Are tandems still made?

In recent years there has been a revival of interest in both racing and touring tandems. A wide range of models are available from specialist manufacturers in Britain and in the rest of Europe.

Can riders of different builds ride the same tandem?

There are many combinations of frame sizes. As a tandem handles better if the bigger of the two riders is steersman, a typical size frame would be 23 in (58 cm) front and 21 in (53 cm) rear. Another combination is man's front frame with a top tube and ladies rear frame without. Young children can be carried on the back seat of a tandem if a special set of pedals on short cranks are fitted to the seat tube.

Can tandems go faster than solo machines?

A tandem is considerably faster than a solo, for although it is not a great deal heavier it is propelled by twice the muscle power.

Why do some adults ride tricycles?

Some cyclists turn to three-wheel machines because they have balance problems. But most tricyclists ride because there is a certain appeal about these slightly eccentric machines. A tricycle makes an ideal commuting mount because it can be halted at road junctions and traffic lights without the rider putting a foot to the ground. Tricycles are safe when roads are icy, and motorists tend to give them more space when overtaking. There are even enthusiasts who race on tricycles, although they go appreciably slower than solo machines.

Is a tricycle easier to ride than a two-wheel machine?

Even experienced cyclists require a good deal of practice before they are able to ride a tricycle safely. This is basically because cornering technique is completely different. When turning left a two-wheeler rider instinctively leans to the left. But on a tricycle the rider's weight must be moved to the left (it is not enough to just lean to the left) otherwise the left hand rear wheel will lift off the ground.

Can a conventional cycle be converted to a tricycle?

Yes, there is a conversion kit available that bolts onto the rear triangle of a conventional frame. The frame can later be restored to two-wheel use if required.

2

THE FRAME

What is the most popular frame design?

Apart from small-wheel and folding machines, all bicycles have
the same basic frame design – the traditional 'diamond' frame –
made up of triangles. The rear triangle is formed by the seat
tube, chainstays and seatstays, and the front triangle by the seat,
top and down tubes.

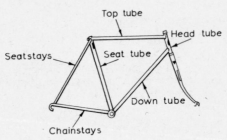

Fig. 6. *The main frame tubes*

What is lug construction?

Where frame tubes join they are brazed into lugs. A lug set
comprises top and bottom head lugs, seat lug and bottom
bracket shell. Seatstays are brazed onto the seat lug, front and
rear fork ends are brazed into slots in the fork blades, seat and
chainstays. Lugless 'welded' frames are also made, although not
considered to be as strong as the conventional type.

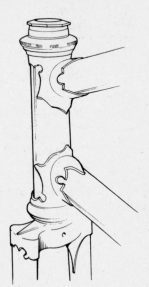

Fig. 7. Head lugs and fork crown

Fig. 8. Cutaway view of head lug showing
how frame tubes are mitred so that they
butt together accurately

What materials are used?

Cheaper frames are built with seamed high-carbon tubing, while good quality lightweight frames are built with seamless drawn tubing made from special alloy steels. The best lightweight tubing is made by TI-Reynolds of Birmingham whose Reynolds '531' manganese molybdenum alloy steel tubing is the most popular material for frame building with both British and overseas frame makers. Reynolds also manufacture '753' tubing.

A very light gauge and even lighter in weight than 531, it is supplied to only a few Reynolds-approved frame builders, and its use is restricted to specialised racing frames.

What is double butted frame tubing?

This is the Reynolds invention which made today's lightweight frames possible. The cold drawn seamless tubes are thicker at each end, where the stresses are greatest, while the outside diameter remains constant. The lesser thickness in the middle of the tube saves weight and ensures a resilient and responsive frame.

How is it possible to tell if a frame is made from Reynolds tubing?

It will be indicated by a transfer about the size of a postage stamp on the seat tube and fork blades. Study the transfer carefully to see if the frame is made from plain gauge or butted tubing, and if

Fig. 9. Ladies sports model with 'mixte' frame

the whole frame, including forks and seat and chainstays, is made from Reynolds tubing or just the three main frame tubes. The transfer can also help to date an old frame; transfers issued before July 1973 did not carry the company's name and address.

Is the ladies frame without a top tube in any way inferior to the man's frame?

Ladies frames are neither as rigid nor responsive because of their shape. Another drawback is that brake and gear cables need to be longer and tend to be less responsive to the controls. A good compromise between the two frame designs is the 'mixte', which instead of a single down tube as most ladies frames have, has narrow section twin stays from the top head lug down to the rear fork end. This layout saves weight without reducing rigidity.

How is frame size measured?

The length of the seat tube is taken from the bottom bracket to the top of the seat lug.

Are frame sizes measured in Imperial or metric units?

At present Imperial measurements are generally used by frame builders and frame sizes usually go up in half-inch steps, although frame builders in continental Europe use centimetres; frame sizes go up in ½ cm steps. The smallest practical adult frame is 19½ in (49.5 cm), the largest 25½ in (65 cm).

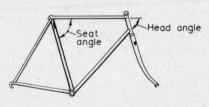

Fig. 10. Frame angles

How is fork rake calculated?

This is the distance between an imaginary line extending down from the head tube and the centre of the front wheel axle. A short rake gives a lively and responsive ride at the expense of a certain amount of comfort.

Fig. 11. How to measure the rake of the forks

Fork rake

What is meant by frame 'clearance'?

The clearance is the distance between the top of the tyre and the front fork crown or rear brake bridge. On touring and utility machines there will be generous clearance to allow space for mudguards to be fitted. Racing frames have minimum clearance to save weight and for rigidity.

How can a cyclist calculate which size the frame should be?

The most popular formula is to take the inside leg measurement and subtract 9 in (230 mm). Thus somebody with a 31 in (790 mm) inside leg would require a 22 in (560 mm) frame. Another method is to divide height by three. So that a six-footer (1.8 m) would have a 24 in (610 mm) frame.

What are the advantages of having a frame made to measure?

Although it costs considerably more than a frame bought ready built, experienced cyclists feel it is worthwhile to have a frame tailored to their precise requirements.

12

A specialist frame builder will take the customer's measurements, will ask what type of cycling the frame will be used for – racing, touring, or both – and will want to know if any special brazed-on fittings are required, such as pump pegs, bottle cage eyes and cable eyes. He will also discuss the various types of rear fork ends, either the forward-facing ends, available with a lug to carry a derailleur gear if required, or more rarely, rear-facing ends used mainly on frames intended for track racing. He should then be able to supply a frame of exactly the right dimensions and geometry to meet the rider's needs.

Another advantage is that most specialist builders offer a very wide range of colour finishes and chromium plating.

What are the advantages of chromium plating on a frame?

It looks good, will not chip, and if fork ends are plated the wheel nuts have a hard surface on which to clamp, reducing the risk of a wheel being pulled over.

3

THE TRANSMISSION

Do gears make cycling any easier?

Gears enable the rider to cope with all types of terrain and weather. When faced with a hill, or riding into a headwind, the rider can engage a lower gear. Speed will probably drop, but pedalling will be possible without undue effort. In favourable conditions, with the wind behind and the road downhill, the rider can take full advantage by engaging high gear.

What is the ideal number of gears for a bicycle?

It depends upon the type of riding undertaken. A single freewheel is more than adequate for short journeys where there are not too many hills. For slightly more demanding types of riding there are three and five speed hub gears. And for the enthusiast who wants to cover considerable distances there are five or ten gears, five being sufficient for most purposes. However, racing cyclists taking part in long distance road races, and tourists who want to take in hill country or mountains, will need ten or twelve close ratio gears, in order that rhythm is maintained when passing through the gears.

What factors affect the gear ratio?

A large chainwheel and a small rear sprocket will give a high gear. A small chainwheel and a large sprocket will give a low gear.

For example, a tourist climbing a very hilly terrain loaded up with panniers etc. might have a chainwheel with 42 teeth and rear sprocket with 22 teeth, this will give him a gear of 51.5 in if

	36	38	40	42	44	45	46	47	48	49	50	51	52	53	54	55	56	57
12	81.0	85.5	90.0	94.5	99.0	101.2	103.5	105.8	108.0	110.2	112.5	114.7	117.0	119.2	121.5	123.7	126.0	128.1
13	74.8	78.9	83.1	87.2	91.4	93.4	95.5	97.6	99.7	101.8	103.9	105.9	108.0	110.0	112.1	114.2	116.3	118.3
14	69.5	73.3	77.1	81.0	84.9	86.8	88.7	90.6	92.6	94.5	96.4	98.3	100.3	102.2	104.1	106.0	108.0	109.9
15	64.8	68.4	72.0	75.6	79.2	81.0	82.8	84.6	86.4	88.2	90.0	91.8	93.6	95.4	97.2	99.0	100.8	102.6
16	60.8	64.2	67.5	70.9	74.3	75.9	77.6	79.3	81.0	82.7	84.4	86.0	87.8	89.4	91.1	92.8	94.5	96.1
17	57.2	60.4	63.6	66.7	69.9	71.5	73.1	74.6	76.2	77.8	79.4	81.0	82.6	84.2	85.7	87.3	88.9	90.5
18	54.0	57.0	60.0	63.0	66.0	67.5	69.0	70.5	72.0	73.5	75.0	76.5	78.0	79.5	81.0	82.5	84.0	85.5
19	51.2	54.0	56.8	59.7	62.5	64.0	65.4	66.8	68.2	69.6	71.1	72.4	73.9	75.3	76.7	78.2	79.5	81.0
20	48.6	51.3	54.0	56.7	59.4	60.7	62.1	63.4	64.8	66.2	67.5	68.8	70.2	71.5	72.9	74.2	75.6	76.9
21	46.3	48.9	51.4	54.0	56.6	57.8	59.2	60.4	61.7	63.0	64.3	65.5	66.9	68.2	69.4	70.7	72.0	73.3
22	44.2	46.6	49.1	51.5	54.0	55.2	56.5	57.6	58.9	60.1	61.4	62.6	63.8	65.0	66.2	67.5	68.7	69.9
23	42.3	44.6	47.0	49.3	51.6	52.8	54.0	55.2	56.3	57.5	58.7	59.8	61.0	62.2	63.4	64.5	65.7	66.9
24	40.5	42.7	45.0	47.3	49.5	50.6	51.8	52.9	54.0	55.1	56.3	57.3	58.5	59.6	60.7	61.8	63.0	64.1
25	38.9	41.1	43.2	45.4	47.5	48.6	49.7	50.8	51.8	52.9	54.0	55.1	56.2	57.2	58.3	59.4	60.4	61.6
26	37.4	39.5	41.5	43.6	45.7	46.7	47.8	48.8	49.9	50.9	51.9	53.0	54.0	55.0	56.1	57.2	58.1	59.2
27	36.0	38.0	40.0	42.0	44.0	45.0	46.0	47.0	48.0	49.0	50.0	51.0	52.0	53.0	54.0	55.0	56.0	57.0
28	34.8	36.6	38.6	40.5	42.4	43.4	44.4	45.3	46.3	47.2	48.2	49.2	50.1	51.1	52.0	53.0	54.0	55.0
29	33.5	35.4	37.2	39.1	41.0	41.9	42.8	43.7	44.7	45.6	46.5	47.5	48.4	49.4	50.3	51.2	52.1	53.1
30	32.4	34.2	36.0	37.8	39.6	40.5	41.4	42.2	43.2	44.1	45.0	45.9	46.8	47.7	48.6	49.5	50.4	51.3
31	31.3	33.1	34.8	36.6	38.4	39.2	40.1	40.9	41.8	42.7	43.6	44.4	45.3	46.2	47.0	47.9	48.8	49.7

Fig. 12. Calculating gear ratio for 27 in wheels. The top line represents the number of teeth on the chainwheel, the left-hand column represents the number of teeth on the rear sprocket. Where columns and lines meet gives the gear ratio in inches

his bicycle has 27 in wheels (smaller wheels would mean a lower gear). At the other extreme, a racing cyclist descending a mountain pass in the Tour de France might be pedalling a top gear of 54-tooth chainwheel and 12-tooth rear sprocket, giving a gear of 121.5 in.

What is a suitable gear ratio for normal riding?

Depending upon the fitness of the individual, something in the region of 70 to 80 in is a 'normal' gear, say a 48-tooth chainwheel and 18-tooth rear sprocket for a ratio of 72 in.

Why is the gear ratio of a bicycle expressed in inches?

This practice goes back to the days of the penny farthing bicycle with its big front wheel and tiny rear. The diameter of the front wheel governed how many inches the cycle travelled with one revolution of the pedals, which were direct drive to the hub. Although the penny farthing disappeared almost a hundred years ago we still retain the same idea today.

How is gear ratio calculated on a modern bicycle?

Either by consulting a gear chart (p. 15), or by the formula

$$\frac{\text{number of teeth on chainwheel}}{\text{number of teeth on rear sprocket}} \times \text{diameter of rear wheel}$$

A typical example would be

$$\frac{48 \text{ teeth}}{18 \text{ teeth}} \times 27 \text{ inches} = 71.9 \text{ inches}$$

How many types of gear system are available?

Although numerous gearing systems have been invented over the years, there are only two in general use today – hub gears, usually fitted to utility machines, and derailleur gears, usually fitted to sports models. The hub gear mechanism is totally enclosed in the rear hub, and is available in three or five-speed form. The derailleur gear – so called by its French inventor because it changes gear by 'derailling' the chain from one sprocket to another – provides five or six gears, doubling up to ten or twelve gears if used with a double chainwheel.

What are the pros and cons of the two gear change systems?

The hub gear is the heavier and more robust of the two. It provides fewer gear ratios and it is not possible to get closely spaced ratios. However, as the mechanism in enclosed in the hub it is protected from water and dirt, and requires little maintenance. However, when a mechanical fault does occur it usually needs to be dealt with by a specialist repairer.

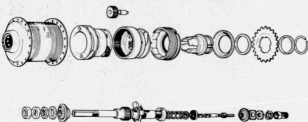

Fig. 13. Exploded view of a Sturmey-Archer three-speed hub gear

The derailleur offers a large humber of combinations of gear ratios. As the mechanism is attached to the rear fork end, it is more vulnerable to damage. On the other hand adjustments and repairs can be carried out with a minimum of mechanical knowledge.

What are the differences between ratios on Sturmey-Archer hub gears?

For three-speed gears they are: low gear, decrease of 25%; normal gear, direct drive; high gear, increase of 33⅓%. For

17

five-speed gears: super low gear, decrease of 33⅓%; low gear, decrease of 21.1%; normal gear, direct drive; high gear, increase of 26.6%; super high gear, increase of 50%.

Do all derailleur gears have the same type of mechanism?

Although mechanisms are available in a wide range of prices and materials, including steel, aluminium alloy, nylon and titanium, they all work on the same principle. A distorting parallelogram moves the gear arm inwards and outwards, guiding the chain from one freewheel sprocket to another. The mechanism is cable operated. Pulling the gear lever back moves the gear arm inwards. A forward push of the lever moves the arm outwards.

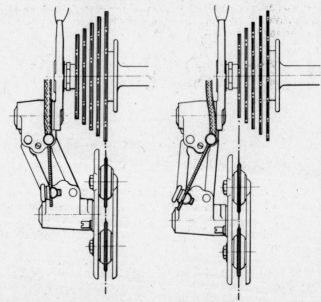

Fig. 14. In bottom gear the de-railleur gear arm should be in line with the largest sprocket

Fig. 15. In top gear the derailleur gear arm should be parallel to the smallest sprocket

Is it possible to change gear at any time?

A hub gear can be changed whether the cycle is stationary or in motion. It is possible to change a derailleur gear only when the chainset is in motion.

Fig. 16. Handlebar mounted gear control lever

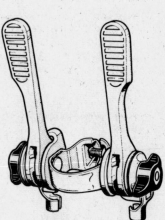

Fig. 17. Down tube mounted gear control twin levers

Where on the cycle are the gear control levers fitted?

Hub gear control levers are mounted on the handlebars or incorporated in a handlebar 'twist-grip'. The usual position for derailleur levers is at the top of the down tube. Other positions are in the ends of the handlebars or on the handlebar stem.

19

What is meant by close and wide ratio gears?

Close ratio means there is only a small step between each gear. A road racing cyclist would use close ratios with one tooth difference between each sprocket size. A typical close ratio freewheel would be 13–14–15–16–17 teeth. Wide ratio gears would be used by a rider with less specialised requirements, such as a long-distance tourist. A typical freewheel would be 14–16–18–21–24 teeth.

What are the largest and smallest practical sprocket sizes?

The smallest is 12 teeth, useful where there is a descent or strong following wind. The largest is 34 teeth, which would be used by a heavily laden tourist in mountainous country. However, to cope with sprockets of this size a gear with a specially long arm is needed. Most standard mechanisms can accommodate sprockets of up to 28 teeth.

How many sprockets can be screwed on to a multiple freewheel?

The most popular number of sprockets for touring and sports use is five. However, six sprockets (giving 12 gears with a double chainset) are frequently used by racing cyclists. The latest

Fig. 18. The freewheel body and sprockets

Fig. 19. The assembled freewheel

development in multiple freewheels is a seven speed developed by a Japanese manufacturer. Each type requires its own five, six or seven speed freewheel body, and the seven speed also needs a special narrow section chain.

20

How is a multiple freewheel removed from a hub?

A special freewheel tool is needed. Depending on the type of freewheel, it will be splined or have two pegs that fit into corresponding slots in the freewheel body. The hub axle fits through the remover which is held in place by tightening the wheel nut. Using a spanner turn the remover anticlockwise a quarter of a turn. Then slacken off the wheel nut. Repeat the process until the freewheel has fully unscrewed. As an alternative to using a spanner, the remover can be gripped in a vice.

What is a fixed wheel?

A single sprocket screwed direct onto the rear hub giving a direct drive. An advantage of the fixed wheel is that during winter it is less susceptible to bad weather, road salt and other hazards that can attack a derailleur mechanism.

How is a fixed wheel sprocket removed from a hub?

The first step is to unscrew the locking ring. It has a left-hand thread, so unscrews clockwise. A simple chain tool consisting of a steel bar with a length of chain attached near one end is used to unscrew the sprocket. Fit the end of the bar between two teeth and wrap the chain anticlockwise round the sprocket, then pull on the bar to unscrew the sprocket clockwise. Use the tool to fully tighten the replacement sprocket before fitting the locking ring.

What type of riding is the fixed wheel used for?

It is popular with racing cyclists in their off-season training. Because there is no possibility of freewheeling it offers the discipline of continuous pedalling at a higher rate than would be necessary with a freewheel. The fixed wheel is also used in track racing where the effort is usually short and explosive and the rider needs a strong and positive transmission.

How many brakes are required on a bicycle equipped with a fixed wheel?

One only; as the drive is direct it is possible to slow down by back pedalling. The law requires a bicycle to have two independent braking systems, and as a fixed wheel is regarded as one system it can be ridden with a front brake only.

What is a spoke protector?

A metal or plastic disc that fits onto the hub under the freewheel. It covers the bottom ends of the spokes, protecting them if the gear arm should get out of adjustment and swing over into the wheel.

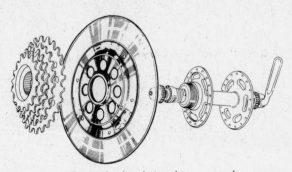

Fig. 20. A nylon spoke disc designed to prevent the gear arm fouling the spokes in the rear wheel

By how much do gears increase the cost of a cycle?

A cycle with a three-speed hub gear will cost about £5 more than a single-speed. Sports models are usually available in five or ten-speed versions, a ten-speed costing £5 to £6 more.

What are the likely causes of derailleur gears slipping?

If the chain slips over the teeth of the freewheel sprockets check for signs of wear, such as 'hooked' teeth or a sloppy chain. If the chain jumps from one sprocket to another without warning, the probable cause is a loose gear lever. Tighten the lever centre screw.

What should be checked if the chain overrides the smallest or largest sprockets?

Check the extent of inward and outward travel of the gear arm which is controlled by two adjusting screws. Tighten the screws until the upper pulley wheel is in line with the sprockets.

Is there a standard size bicycle chain?

Two sizes are in general use, $\frac{1}{2} \times \frac{3}{32}$ in on derailleur equipped machines, $\frac{1}{2} \times \frac{1}{8}$ in on single or three-speed machines.

When should a chain be replaced?

It depends on the mileage it has covered, but a chain in average use would last about two years. As a chain wears out it becomes sloppy and will not bed down properly on the teeth of the chainwheel or freewheel. In extreme cases the chain will fail to grip the teeth, particularly when used with a newer freewheel.

How can the chain be removed?

If the chain is $\frac{1}{2} \times \frac{1}{8}$ look for the connecting link, which is held in place by a spring clip. The clip can be prised off by a screwdriver or pliers.

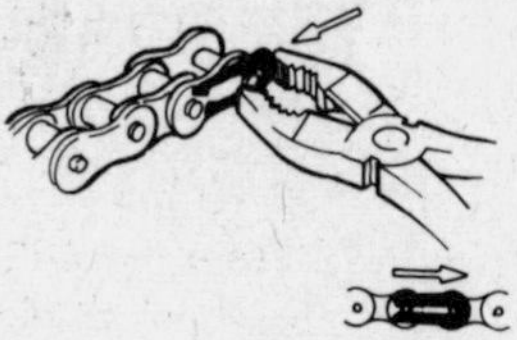

Fig. 21. Pliers are the best tool for removing and fitting chain spring links. When fitted, such a link should always have its closed end facing the normal direction of rotation

A ½ × ³/₃₂ chain when used on a multiple freewheel does not have a connecting link (it would catch the closely-spaced freewheel sprockets), and is broken by a special tool called a rivet extractor. This is like a miniature vice that clamps the chain, and when the handle is turned the rivet is forced out. The same job can be done using a hammer and punch but it is quite tricky and can result in damage to the chain.

How tight should the chain be?

A chain should have about ½ in (12 mm) up-and-down movement at its midpoint on a non-derailleur machine. Tightness is adjusted by moving the back wheel forwards or backwards in the rear fork ends. On a derailleur-equipped machine chain tension is regulated by the gear arm. The chain will be longer than for a single speed, but the arm should not have to take up so much tension that it goes back until it catches on the freewheel.

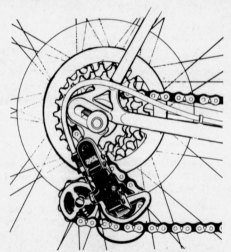

Fig. 22. If the chain is too long the gear pulley arm will fold back on itself

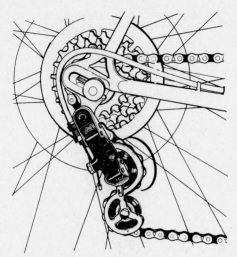

*Fig. 23. Shortening the chain pulls the gear pulley
arm forward to the correct angle*

What is meant by chain line?

The chain should travel in an absolutely straight line between the
chainwheel and rear sprocket. If the sprocket is out of line it is
adjusted by placing packing washers on the hub. On a derailleur
with its five rear sprockets, the chain line can only be correct in
one gear – when the chain is engaged on the middle sprocket. In
all other gears there is some distortion, which is why there may
be some difficulty in riding with the chain on the largest
chainwheel and smallest sprocket or largest sprocket and
smallest chainwheel.

What parts make up the chainset?

The two pedal cranks and the chainwheel (or chainwheels in the
case of a double chainset).

What materials are used?

In most cases steel for utility models and aluminium alloy for lightweights.

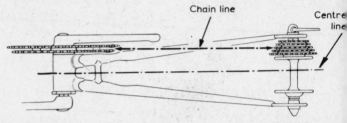

Fig. 24. Chain alignment. The chain line should be parallel to the centre line when the chain is on the middle sprocket of a five-speed freewheel

What are the advantages and drawbacks of the two materials?

A steel chainset is only a fraction of the cost of one made from aluminium alloy. It will stand up to rough treatment and will last almost indefinitely. The major disadvantage of steel is its weight; aluminium alloy is far lighter and the weight saving considerable on a component such as a double chainset.

What is meant by a 'detachable chainset'?

The chainwheels (which are also called chainrings) are bolted to the crank arms for easy removal when altering gear ratios. On cheaper sets the chainwheel is permanently attached to the crank, making it necessary to change the complete chainset assembly to alter gear ratio.

How are cranks fitted to the bottom bracket axle?

Steel cranks are fastened with steel cotter pins. These are flatted pins, threaded at one end. They are wedged against a flat on the bottom bracket axle and secured by a nut. 'Cotterless' aluminium alloy cranks are bolted onto the square end of a matching bottom bracket axle.

What are the standard lengths of cranks?

On utility machines the usual crank length for an adult is 6½ in (165 mm). Cranks on lightweight machines are usually 6¾ in (170 mm) long, although tall riders sometimes fit 7 in (175 mm) cranks.

What types of chainguard are available?

The traditional pattern of chainguard is clipped to the chain stay and seat tube, covering most of the top length of the chain. Some lightweights are equipped with a steel or aluminium alloy chainguard in the shape of a disc bolted to the outside of the chainset.

When should cotter pins be replaced?

The tell-tale signs of worn or ill-fitting cotter pins are creaking noises that come from the cranks every time pressure is applied

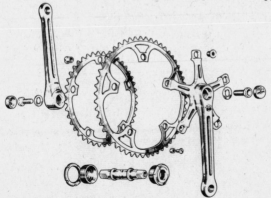

Fig. 25. Expoded view of a typical alloy cotterless double chainset complete with bottom bracket axle and cups

27

on the pedals, or cranks dropping forward slightly with every revolution. To rectify, knock the pin further in with a hammer and tighten the nut. If the pin goes so far in that the head is flush with the crank a new pin is needed.

How are cotter pins fitted and removed?

To fit, push the pin into the hole in the crank with the flat face of the pin facing the flat on the bottom bracket axle. The pin should push in far enough for the head to protrude from the crank by about ¼ in (6 mm). It can then be driven home with a hammer and the nut tightened. Cotter pins are made slightly over size. If it is a tight fit the flat should be filed until it can be pushed in. To remove, unscrew the nut and knock the pin out with a hammer. When using a hammer the crank should always be supported on a block of wood.

What special tools are needed to remove and fit cotterless cranks?

A crank puller, a crank locknut spanner and an allen key (to fit the dust cap).

How are the cranks removed and fitted?

To remove, unscrew the dust cap and crank locknut and remove the washer. Screw the crank puller into the crank, taking care

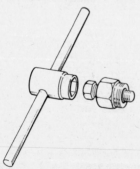

Fig. 26. Special tool for fitting and removing alloy cotterless cranks

not to cross the threads. Also ensure it is screwed all the way in, otherwise it can strip the soft crank threads. Slowly screw the bolt into the puller. It will push against the end of the bottom bracket axle, forcing the crank off. If the crank is wedged firmly on do not strain on the puller, instead tap the crank with a mallet.

To fit, place the crank on the square end of the bottom bracket axle, tighten the locknut, and replace the dust cap. Cotterless cranks have a habit of working loose; if this is a recurring problem, protect the crank with a piece of wood and tap it into the axle.

What are the signs of a worn bottom bracket bearing?

A rough grinding feel when the bottom bracket axle is turned.

What tools are required to strip down and assemble the bottom bracket?

A 'C' spanner to fit the lockring that screws onto the left-hand bottom bracket cup, a peg spanner, with two raised pegs that slot into the holes in the left-hand bottom bracket cup, and an adjustable spanner for the right-hand (chainwheel side) bottom bracket cup. In an emergency a soft metal punch can be substituted for the 'C' spanner and peg spanner.

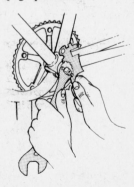

Fig. 27. Adjusting the bottom bracket. Grip the adjusting cup with the peg spanner and tighten the lockring with the 'C' spanner

29

Which is the 'adjusting' and which is the 'fixed' bottom bracket cup?

The left-hand cup adjusts by screwing in or out until the bottom bracket axle turns freely without any play. It has a right-hand thread, tightening up in a clockwise direction. The right-hand cup is 'fixed', and is only removed if in need of replacement. It has a left-hand thread, tightening up anticlockwise.

How is the bottom bracket stripped down?

After removing the cranks slacken off the lockring with the 'C' spanner. Then unscrew the adjusting cup with the peg spanner. It should now be possible to slide the bottom bracket axle and ball bearings out of the bottom bracket shell.

How is it possible to say which bottom bracket parts need replacing?

Clean oil and grease from the cups, axle and ball bearings, and examine them closely. If there are any items showing signs of pitting they should be replaced. There are various types of cups, and axles are made in varying lengths, so when buying replacements it is advisable to take the originals along as a pattern. Most bottom brackets take 11 ¼ in ball bearings in each cup.

How is the bottom bracket assembled?

Lay the cycle on its side (fixed cup down). Grease the fixed cup and place the bearings in the grease. Before fitting the adjusting cup, grease it, put the bearings in place, and slip the cup onto the short end of the axle (the long end will be needed to accommodate the chainwheel).

Holding cup and axle together so that no bearings fall out carefully lower the axle into the bottom bracket shell until the axle flange rests on the bearings in the fixed cup. Tighten the adjusting cup until the axle is turning smoothly. Secure the cup by tightening the lockring.

What are the main types of pedal?

Pedals with rubber treads are fitted to utility machines, metal (or alloy) 'rat-trap' type to lightweights. Metal pedals are narrower and can be fitted with toe-clips.

Do pedal spindles have a standard thread?

The standard British thread is $\frac{9}{16}$ in × 20 tpi, but the left-hand pedal has a left-hand thread and the right-hand pedal a right-hand thread. They are usually stamped 'L' or 'R' on the spindle end.

The usual length of thread is 9 mm, although some pedals have 13 mm of thread for thicker section aluminium alloy cranks. Care should be taken to avoid damaging soft threads when screwing steel pedals into alloy cranks.

What is the function of toe-clips and straps?

They greatly increase pedalling efficiency. The toe-clip bolts onto the front of the pedal, and the strap which loops round the foot, is threaded through the pedal side plates and the slot in the toe-clip. In addition to the pedal being pushed down on the downwards stroke, toe-clips make it possible for a double action with the pedal pulled up on the upwards stroke.

Are toe-clips available in different sizes?

They should fit snugly on the toe of the shoe, and are made in three lengths, short, medium and long.

What are shoeplates?

Slotted plates made from alloy or nylon that are screwed or nailed to the soles of cycling shoes under the ball of the foot. The back of the pedal fits into the slot so that the plate can assist with the pulling action on the upward stroke. Plates are used universally by racing cyclists.

Is there not a safety hazard in having the feet strapped and clamped into the pedals?

Toe-straps have special quick-release buckles which allow them to be slackened off with a flick of the thumb. In congested traffic conditions where the rider needs to put his feet to the ground at frequent intervals, he soon gains the knack of disengaging his shoeplate from the pedal when necessary.

4

WHEELS AND TYRES

What are the standard sizes of wheel rims?

26 × 1⅜ in for utility machines, 26 × 1¼ in for sports models of 19½ in or smaller, 27 × 1¼ in or 1 in for all other sizes of sports model.

What are the pros and cons of steel and alloy rims?

Chromium plated steel rims are strong and durable. Rims made from aluminium alloy are rather more fragile, but they are lighter, will not rust, and provide a better braking surface, particularly in wet weather.

How many spokes are there in a cycle wheel?

Until recently British bicycles had 32 spokes in the front wheel and 40 in the rear. But in recent years many manufacturers have changed to the Continental practice of building both wheels with 36 spokes.

Racing wheels are often built with fewer spokes to save weight, 28/28 is common, and in especially favourable conditions 24/24 can be used.

Why was the change from 32/40 made?

Largely as a matter of convenience for the cycle industry. It made sense to have more spokes in the rear wheel, which has to carry more weight than the front, but it meant manufacturers had to carry stocks of both front and rear rims. The 36/36 is a compromise that allows interchangeability between wheels and between British and Continental manufacturers.

What are butted spokes?

Better quality spokes which are thicker at the ends. A typical plain spoke would be 14 gauge, a butted spoke 14/16 gauge.

Why do racing cyclists favour large-flange hubs?

A racing cyclist wants equipment that will absorb only a minimum amount of his energy; a large-flange hub means a shorter spoke length and a more rigid and responsive wheel. However small-flange hubs give a more comfortable ride.

Fig. 28. Large-flange (left) and small flange (right) rear hubs

How are hubs fixed into the frame?

By two methods, track nuts or a quick-release mechanism. The former are hexagon nuts (5/16 inch front, 3/8 inch rear) with integral serrated washers for maximum grip. The quick-release is a cam-action mechanism that clamps the hub into the fork-end by a single turn of a lever.

What are the advantages and disadvantages of the two systems?

Track nuts are cheaper and are used with a solid axle that is slightly stronger than the hollow axle needed for quick-release. Quick-release hubs can be fitted and removed without the use of a spanner. They were first developed for racing cyclists needing a rapid wheel change after a puncture, but are equally useful to the cyclist who frequently removes wheels to carry his machine by car or public transport.

What is meant by single and double-sided hubs?

A single-sided hub is threaded on one side to take either a freewheel or single fixed sprocket. If the hub is double-sided it will have two threads, on one side for a freewheel, and on the other for a fixed sprocket. Double-sided fixed wheel hubs are also used.

How is a wheel 'trued'?

The wheel is made to run true by gradually tightening and freeing the brass nipples that fix the spokes into the rim, tensioning and slackening spokes until the rim is pulled central. When the job is completed the protruding ends of the spokes inside the rim should be filed off as they can puncture the inner tube.

Why do spokes sometimes snap?

Usually because too much tension is on the spokes at one point. Another cause could be a stripped nipple thread. Replacing a single broken spoke is a fairly simple job and in an emergency can be carried out without removing the wheel from the frame. However, if the broken spoke is on the 'gear side' of the hub it will be necessary to take out the wheel and remove the freewheel before the spoke end can be pulled out.

If the wheel is severely buckled or several spokes are broken it is a job best left to a specialist repairer.

What is a 'dished' wheel?

A rear wheel that has been built with the rim 'off centre' to the hub so that the extra width of a multi-freewheel can be accommodated.

When should hub bearings be adjusted?

Hubs should be checked at least once a month for play or tightness in the bearings. If the bearing is too loose it will be possible to rock the axle from side to side in the hub. If the bearing is tight the wheel will not spin freely (the test is to lift the wheel off the ground with the valve at the top, the weight of the valve should be sufficient to carry the wheel round). Special thin section spanners

Locknut Cone Washer Dustcap Axle

Fig. 29. Exploded view of front hub axle

are needed to adjust the bearing cones, one to hold the cones, the other for the locknut. When the cone has been adjusted so that the axle spins freely without any play, it should be fixed in place by tightening the locknut against it.

What is the difference between wired-on and tubular tyres?

The wired-on tyre has a separate inner tube and rim tape and is made with wired edges to enable it to seat into the rim. Tubulars have a lightweight latex inner tube sewn inside the outer cover.

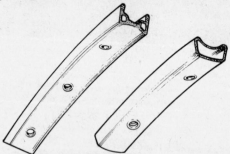

Fig. 30. Rim shapes. High-pressure rims (left) have a deep section to accommodate wired-on tyres. Sprint rims (right) are shallower, giving a wide bed on which tubular tyres are fixed with adhesive

They can only be fitted to 'sprint' rims, and are secured with special rubber-based cement.

What are the main uses of the two types of tyre?

Wired-ons are available in a wide range of weights and tread patterns and are used for all types of cycling except racing. Tubulars, which are about one third the weight of wired-ons, are universally used for racing.

Are tubulars suitable for touring use?

Heavier tubulars, say 15 oz (420 g), are frequently fitted to touring machines. But because of their thin layer of tread they tend to puncture more easily than wired-ons. When a wired-on punctures it is a simple matter to repair it or fit a spare inner tube. Because the tubular's inner tube is sewn inside the outer cover it is impossible to carry out a roadside repair. Instead it is necessary to carry several spare tyres.

How many valve types are in use on British made cycles?

Three types: The Woods valve, usually found on utility machines; the Schrader, found on both utility and sports machines, and the Presta valve, for use with 'high pressure' tyres and tubes on sports machines, and on tubulars.

The valve rubber on Woods-type valves has today generally been superseded by a replaceable insert. Schrader valves are the same type as used on car tyres and will take either a conventional cycle pump or a car pump. Presta valves have a plunger with a knurled lock nut that must be unscrewed before the pump can be attached.

What are the relative merits of butyl and rubber inner tubes?

Butyl tubes are preferred by most cycle manufacturers. Their main advantage is that they retain their pressure almost indefinitely and tyres need inflating at infrequent intervals.

Rubber tubes are lighter and give a slightly more lively ride. However they do allow a certain amount of air to seep out, and tyre pressures regularly require 'topping up'.

What is the recommended pressure for cycle tyres?

For general riding 70 lb/in^2 (p.s.i) (6 atm) is recommended. If roads are icy or wet, pressure should be reduced. It can be increased if the cycle is heavily laden. Tubulars are inflated to higher pressures, and a racing cyclist on a smooth track will have his tyres at about 100 lb/in^2 (7.5 atm).

What is the function of the rim tape?

It is a cloth or plastic tape that fits into the well of the rim to protect the inner tube from any sharp edges on the spoke nipples or spoke ends.

How is the pump coupled up to the valve?

Either by a flexible connector that screws onto the valve or by a push-on adapter. A standard cycle pump will inflate any type of tube, but the connector used depends on the valve type, Presta, Woods or Schrader all being different diameters. The push-on adapter is permanently attached to the pump end, and is used exclusively with Presta valves.

Where is the pump carried?

Usually on the top of the down tube or front of the seat tube. More rarely behind the seat tube or beneath the top tube. The pump is held in place by brazed-on pegs or screw-on clips.

How are wired-on tyres fitted and removed?

To fit the tyre, slip one edge over the the rim, pump a little air into the inner tube, and fit the valve into its hole in the rim, screwing on the rim washer to hold it in place. Then, tucking the tube into the cover as you go, start from the valve and run the hands round the tyre, easing it on to the rim. Take care to avoid pinching the tube between tyre and rim. When the tyre is in place inflate to about half pressure and spin the wheel to check that the tyre has bedded down into the well of the rim and is running true.

What is the best method of fitting tubulars?

Tubulars are stuck onto a flat rim bed, unlike wired-on tyres that fit into a deep-welled rim. Several proprietary brands of cement are available for sticking tyres, but do not use rubber solution which is unsuitable. To fit the tyre, start by inserting the valve in the rim, and work the hands round the tyre, stretching it onto the rim. This operation needs some care if the tyre walls are not to get smeared with cement. After fitting and partial inflation the tyre will almost certainly need 'squaring up' on the rim; use the edge of the base tape as a guide.

Which is the best way to carry a spare tubular?

Carefully fold the tubular so that the tread is on the outside of the fold with the valve facing in. A tubular is particularly vulnerable to chafing, and should be wrapped in thick paper or polythene and then in the cape roll. It can then be strapped to the back of the saddle or to the top of the saddle bag. The same applies to carrying a spare inner tube for wired-on tyres, many cyclists preferring to take a spare rather than bother with a road-side puncture repair.

What is a flint catcher?

A flint catcher, made from wire or alloy, is attached to the brake bolt with a curved bar lightly resting on the tread of the tyre. It pulls thorns, flints or pieces of glass out of the tread before they can penetrate to the inner tube.

5

THE MAIN COMPONENTS

What is the most comfortable type of saddle?

The rider is less likely to suffer problems of saddle soreness if a sports type is used rather than the sprung mattress type. Although the sports saddle is narrower and harder it provides better support than a softer saddle with a minimum of friction.

Why has the plastics saddle become more popular than the traditional leather saddle in recent years?

Although leather saddles can be extremely comfortable and will last for many years, they need a certain amount of 'breaking in' when new. This involves riding on the new saddle, sometimes for several thousand miles, and treating it with a leather dressing, until it has softened and become moulded to the rider's shape.

Plastics saddles need no such breaking in period. They are also impervious to water and never require any type of dressing. Plastics will not 'breathe' in the same way as leather, and the best plastics saddles are covered with suede or some similar material.

Are saddles made in varying widths?

Saddle width depends upon its usage; a racing cyclist who sits well forward needs less support than a tourist whose more upright position throws more weight onto the saddle. A racing saddle is about 5⅝ inches (143 mm) at its widest point, compared to a touring saddle of 6¼ inches (159 mm). Women have a wider pelvic structure than men and need a wider saddle of about 7 inches (178 mm).

What are the main types of saddle pillar?

The cheapest pillar, used on utility machines, is made from steel with a plain top which is clamped by the saddle clip. More expensive are the aluminium alloy pillars with their own saddle cradle which are almost universal on lightweight models. Their advantages are light weight and very precise adjustment of saddle angle. Seat pillar diameter depends upon the type of frame tubing, the most common sizes are 26.2, 26.8, 27.0 and 27.2 mm.

What is the most commonly used cycle braking system?

By far the most popular type is the cable operated caliper brake. A few utility models of traditional design retain rod operated brakes, and there is increasing interest in internal expanding hub brakes.

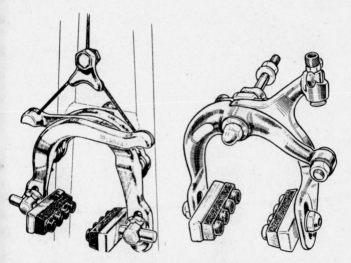

Fig. 31. The two most popular types of cable-operated brakes: left, centre-pull; right, side-pull

Do all caliper brakes work on the same principle?

No, there are two types. Side-pull brakes, in which the cable is clamped to the side of the stirrup, and centre-pull in which the cable operates from a central position above the stirrup.

Are the two systems equally efficient?

Centre-pull brakes are slightly more effective. They do not require as much pressure on the brake levers as side-pulls, they are better balanced and there is less likelihood of the stirrup pulling over to one side and the brake block catching the rim. Side-pulls are lighter, and as there is less cable between stirrup and lever than on centre-pulls they do not feel quite so spongy.

Hub brakes do not seem very popular; is this situation likely to alter?

It is likely that the use of hub brakes will increase, particularly where weight is not the all-important factor, such as on children's and utility models. Safety authorities are unhappy about the

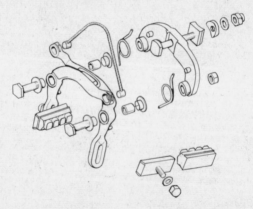

Fig. 32. Exploded view of a centre-pull brake

ineffectiveness of rim brakes in wet weather, and the hub brake operates with the same efficiency in all weathers. Hub brakes have always been rather bulky and heavy but compact designs are being introduced, including a hub brake incorporated in a three-speed gear.

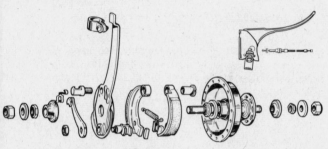

Fig. 33. Exploded view of the Sturmey-Archer hub brake

Why are brakes that operate on the rims less effective in wet weather?

Because a film of water on the rim stops the brake block from gripping properly. This can increase the stopping distance by as much as four times – more if the rims are chromium plated steel.

How can the rider minimise the danger from wet rims?

By gently applying the brakes to clear water from the rims at frequent intervals. Research is being carried out to find the most effective brake blocks in wet conditions, and leather blocks have been found to give a better grip than the conventional rubber or composition blocks.

Which brake is the more effective, front or rear?

The front brake will bring the cycle to a halt most rapidly. But it should be treated with respect. If it is applied too harshly the rider

43

can be thrown over the handlebars. The rear brake is an effective back-up system. This too should be applied gently, otherwise a back wheel skid may result. On long descents the brakes should be applied alternately to avoid rims overheating.

What are hooded brake levers?

The type of levers fitted to dropped handlebars. They are specially shaped to provide a comfortable hand grip as an alternative to resting the hands on the handlebars. On more expensive brakes the levers are usually covered with rubber or plastics hoods to provide a cushion for the hands.

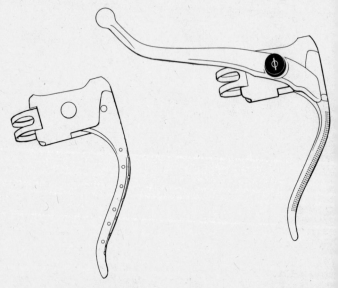

Fig. 34. Hooded brake lever for use on dropped handlebars

Fig. 35. Dual brake lever with additional arm

What is the correct position for hooded levers on dropped handlebars?

The levers should be low enough on the handlebars to be within easy reach of the hands when they are on the bottoms of the bars. Special short reach levers are available for people with small hands. Care should be taken to get the levers exactly level with each other before the handlebars are re-taped.

What happens in an emergency when the hands are positioned on the top of dropped handlebars well away from the brake levers?

Brake levers can be operated from above, with the thumbs resting on the hoods and fingers looped over the levers. Another solution is dual brake levers. These are curved arms that follow the line of the handlebars from the brake levers into the centre of the bars. They can be gripped immediately to apply the brake. A slight drawback is that the stirrups need to be very accurately adjusted as there is only limited travel before the dual levers touch the handlebars. However 'Randonneur' touring handlebars are specially designed with an angled top section for dual levers.

How frequently should brake cables be replaced?

Cables (or inner wires as they are also called) are inexpensive and should be replaced if they become affected by rust or if any of the strands start to fray.

How do I know what type of replacement I need?

Knowing the make and model of brake should be sufficient for the cycle dealer, otherwise take the old cable to the shop.

What are the most common types of cable?

Multi-wire cables housed in plastics sheathed outer casing. A pear-shaped or barrel-shaped nipple slots into the brake lever, the other end of the cable is plain and is clamped into an eye bolt on the brake stirrup.

Should outer casing be replaced at the same time as inner wire?

Not necessarily, although you may prefer to fit new outer casing (which is sold by the yard or metre) if the original is very shabby or rusted inside. Cables should always be greased before fitting.

What is the best way to cut cable and outer casing?

With wire cutters; if blunt cutters or pliers are used they may crimp the outer casing and fray the inner wire.

What route does the brake cable take from the brake lever to the stirrup?

On a man's cycle the rear brake cable will pass through eyelets along the top tube and be routed down the seatstays to the stirrup. The front cable goes direct to the stirrup, passing in front of the handlebars if the handlebar extension is short, behind the handlebars if a longer extension is fitted.

On a ladies machine which does not have a top tube, the cable follows the line of the down tube. It then turns upwards to enter the cable clamp bolt from below.

How can wheels be removed without the tyres catching on the brake blocks?

On better quality brakes there is a quick release device, either on the levers or stirrups. When operated with a flick of the finger it slackens the cable tension, allowing the stirrups to open out enough for the wheels to smoothly pass through. If there is not a quick release it may be necessary to remove one of the brake shoes or to open out the brake stirrup by slackening off the cable clamp bolt.

What should be checked if the front forks vibrate when the front brake is applied?

This is caused by a loose headset. The head fittings are vulnerable to vibration from the forks and need to be regularly checked for play by rocking the bike backwards and forwards with the front brake on and fingers around the headset. Two spanners are needed to adjust the headset. As the home mechanic is unlikely to have the special headset tools the best alternatives are a multi-purpose spanner and an adjustable spanner.

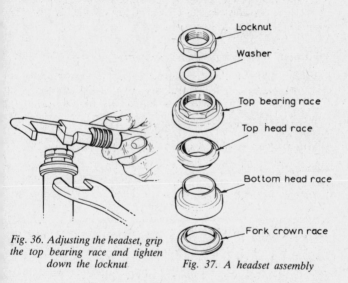

Fig. 36. Adjusting the headset, grip the top bearing race and tighten down the locknut

Fig. 37. A headset assembly

To tighten a loose headset, grip the top bearing race with the adjustable and tighten the top locknut down onto it. Care should be taken not to overtighten the nut as a tight headset is as dangerous as a loose one. If the steering makes a grinding noise when the handlebars are turned, the headset needs to be stripped down and the $5/32$ in ball bearings replaced.

What advantages do dropped handlebars have over straight?

Straight 'all-rounder' handlebars are ideal for short distance riding, but because they can only be gripped at the ends the rider is able to adopt only one position on the bicycle. Dropped handlebars give a more comfortable ride as they provide a variety of hand grips, enabling the rider to frequently change position and ease pressure on arm and back muscles.

In practice the bottoms of the handlebars are used only when the rider is travelling at top speed or battling into a head wind. At other times the hands can rest on the brake levers or in the centre of the handlebars giving an upright position which is best for climbing hills as it aids breathing.

What materials are handlebars made from?

Steel or alloy – the latter being almost universal for sports machines. Alloy handlebars are usually $^{15}/_{16}$ in diameter, with a centre section 1 in diameter where it is clamped into the handlebar stem.

Which dropped handlebar shape is the most popular?

Although fashions come and go the 'Maes' type has been the basic handlebar design for some years now. The 'Maes' shape, which originated in Belgium, has a fairly shallow drop of about 5 in (125 mm), and its square shape provides plenty of alternative hand positions.

Handlebars are made in a wide range of widths and people of particularly large or small stature can choose a wide or narrow bar to match their build.

What are the usual methods of covering dropped handlebars?

They are usually taped. Starting about an inch (25 mm) from the centre of the handlebars the tape is bound round to the handlebar ends where it is secured by push-in plugs (these are also a safety feature to prevent injury from the open handlebar end). Plastics or cloth tape is available, the former is long lasting and looks better than cloth tape. But not everyone likes the feel of plastics, and although cloth needs replacing more frequently it is almost as popular.

An alternative is a sleeve that pulls over the handlebars. This looks good and is very hard wearing. Sleeves are made from leather, suede and foam rubber.

What range of handlebar stem lengths is available?

A typical manufacturer's range would include aluminium alloy stems with forward extensions of 20 mm to 150 mm. These are rather extreme dimensions and most riders would require a stem of between 70 mm and 110 mm. Length is measured from the centre of the expander bolt to the centre line of the handlebars.

How is the stem fixed into the frame?

The bottom of the stem that fits into the fork steerer is slotted. An expander bolt extends down the centre of the stem to a circular tapered wedge which, when the bolt is tightened, pulls up in the slots to open out the stem and fix it firmly in position.

Better quality stems have expander and handlebar clamp bolts with recessed heads which are adjusted by an allen key.

What materials are mudguards made from?

Steel on utility machines, plastics or aluminium on sports machines. Plastics are very light, as is aluminium alloy, which is stronger but more expensive. The most durable mudguards are made from steel, but they are heavy and tend to rattle as the fittings begin to wear.

How are mudguards attached to the cycle?

The front is clamped under the brake nut, and four thick wire stays are bolted to special eyes on the front fork ends. The rear guards also have four stays bolted to the rear fork ends and are fixed by clips to the seat and chainstay bridges.

What are racing mudguards?

This is something of a misnomer as mudguards are never fitted for racing. However many manufacturers fit short mudguards about 12 in (300 mm) long to their sports models. They offer only minimal protection from road spray, and in the UK full-length mudguards are recommended for all types of riding except racing.

Is there any way of recording speed and mileage of a bicycle?

Speedometers are available, either driven off a cable to the front hub or by a nylon pulley on the front tyre. Mileometers have long suffered from being driven by a striker mounted on the spokes, and many people find the continuous ticking an annoyance. A more recent design is silent, with the mileometer driven by a belt to the front hub.

Fig. 38. Mileometer operated by a pulley on the hub

Fig. 39. Speedometer operated by nylon pulley on the front tyre

Have modern materials made any impact on cycle specifications?

Aluminium alloys have been widely used on lightweights for many years, replacing steel for components such as handlebars, chainwheels and rims. Nylon is used in the manufacture of some types of derailleur gear and for saddles. In recent years there has been an accelerating trend towards the use of titanium for key components such as bottom bracket axles, gear pulleys and pedal spindles. Its great strength and lightness make titanium ideal for racing use, the only limitation being high cost.

Have there been any modern innovations in cycle frame materials?

Nothing has yet been found to improve on Reynolds 531 tubing for general racing and touring use. Aluminium frames have gained a certain amount of popularity, but although extremely light, the aluminium tubing cannot be brazed and needs to be joined by bulky lugs. Several manufacturers have built frames made from carbon fibre, but none has gone past the experimental stage.

Is drilling holes in components a practical method of weight saving?

Manufacturers keep weight to a minimum by removing material from such components as the front changer cage, brake levers and chainrings. Some cyclists carry out their own modifications, such as drilling seat pillars, fork ends and cranks. Do-it-yourself drilling done without specialist knowledge can weaken components and is not recommended.

6

FINDING THE RIGHT POSITION

How important is the rider's position on the cycle?

A correct riding position is vital for safety, comfort and maximum efficiency. When experimenting with position the rider should aim for a balance, with the weight evenly distributed between handlebars, saddle and pedals.

What are the symptoms of an unsuitable riding position?

Riding with the saddle too high can lead to strained leg muscles and reduce the rider's control over the machine. A too-low saddle can make cycling hard work. Low handlebars can cause jarred wrists, while adjusting the handlebars too high throws more weight on to the saddle, and can cause saddle soreness.

How can saddle height be determined?

When sitting on the saddle it should just be possible to reach the pedals with the heels, without unduly stretching the legs.

How is the saddle height adjusted?

By freeing the nut and bolt on the seat lug. When raising the saddle it is important to ensure that at least 2 in (50 mm) of saddle pillar remains in the frame. If this is not possible with a standard length seat pillar, the frame is too small.

Can the saddle be adjusted backwards and forwards?

Yes, by loosening the nuts on the saddle clip. Most cyclists find the most comfortable position is with the nose of the saddle about 2½ in (60 mm) behind an imaginary vertical line extending upwards from the bottom bracket.

Should the saddle be tilted up or down?

The saddle should be level, parallel with the top tube. Some riders prefer to have the nose tilted very slightly down, however it should never be tilted back so that the nose is higher than the rear of the saddle.

How do I discover what length handlebar stem I need?

If the elbow is placed against the nose of the saddle it should be possible to touch the handlebars with the tips of the fingers.

How is correct handlebar height determined?

The handlebars (or the tops of dropped handlebars) should be level with the top of the saddle.

Should dropped handlebars be tilted upwards?

Some riders prefer the bottoms of their handlebars to be parallel to the ground but the usual handlebar position is tilted forward about 10°.

What can I do if after following the recommendations on saddle height I still do not feel comfortable on the cycle?

The recommendations are only basic guide lines. It may be necessary to experiment until you find the position that will suit you best. Even the most minor adjustment to riding position feels strange at first, so persevere, ride at least 50 miles (80 km) before deciding whether to make another alteration.

Which part of the foot should rest on the pedal?

Always pedal with the ball of the foot. On pedals with rubber treads it is easy to let the foot slip forward until you are pedalling with the instep. You are not so likely to fall into this habit – which makes for less efficient pedalling – if your cycle is equipped with 'rat-trap' pedals and toe-clips of the appropriate length.

What is ankling?

A pedalling style much advocated a few years ago, and still recommended by some coaches, for smooth pedalling. It involves dropping the heel slightly on the downwards stroke and lifting the heel to give a clawing action on the upward stroke.

7

WHAT TO WEAR

Is it necessary to wear special clothes for cycling?

It depends on how sriously you take your cycling. For short rides of four or five miles (7 or 8 km) normal clothes are quite suitable. Even if your cycling aims are a little more ambitious it is not necessary to go to the expense of buying specialised clothing.

However, when deciding on which clothes to wear, remember that when sitting on a bicycle your back and arms are at almost full stretch, so choose a jacket or sweater that is long in the back, with sleeves of a generous length, otherwise chilly gaps will appear at the waist and wrists.

Are tracksuits suitable wear for cycling?

Tracksuits are ideal, particularly if designed for use with a long top and legs that taper below the knee.

What is the best type of trousers for cycling wear?

Special cycling trousers called plus-twos which end just below the knee with a ribbed elasticated band, and are worn with knee-length socks. Plus-twos have plenty of room at the knee to allow freedom of movement, and are made with a reinforced double seat to cope with wear from the saddle. They are usually made from hard-wearing worsteds, and tend to look neater than tracksuit bottoms which can go baggy after a little wear.

Which types of shorts are most suitable for cycling wear?

Cycling shorts need to be deigned for the job, made from hard-wearing materials, with a reinforced seat. Athletics-type shorts are unsuitable, they are too light and gather up under the crutch.

Why do most cyclists wear braces rather than a belt or elasticated waistband?

A belt or waistband which may be perfectly comfortable for normal wear can become uncomfortably tight after a few miles of cycling. This is because a cyclist's breath fills out the diaphragm rather than the chest.

Do cyclists need to wear socks?

Only the short-distance sprinter can get away without wearing socks. Cycling shoes are light and soft, and quite comfortable without socks, but cycling any distance will lead to blistered feet. White ankle socks look best with shorts, knee-length patterned stockings are usually worn with plus-twos.

What is best to wear on the upper part of the body?

Tracksuit tops and sweaters are the lightest and most comfortable wear for cycling. They do have the drawback of not being windproof and several thin layers of clothing are better than a single thick one. Lightweight nylon jackets are windproof and showerproof but tend to have a Turkish bath effect as the rider warms up. However they can be packed away small enough to fit into a saddle bag. It should be remembered that even when travelling fairly slowly the cyclist creates a cooling breeze, so will require slightly more clothing than would be needed for travelling on foot.

How can the hands be protected from vibration transmitted via the handlebars?

All racing cyclists and many touring cyclists wear track-mitts, special gloves with fingers that end at the first knuckle. They usually have string backs and palms reinforced with a thin layer of foam rubber padding. Racing cyclists also wear them for hand protection in case of a crash.

What types of headgear are available for the cyclist?

In summer a peaked cotton cap to protect the head from the sun is useful. For winter riding some sort of woollen hat should be worn, either the traditional tea cosy pattern or if something more up-to-date is preferred the ski cap and training hats now sold by cycle clothing stockists.

Do cyclists wear crash helmets?

Crash helmets are compulsory for road and track racing in the UK. The helmets are lightweight, made from strips of foam rubber covered with leather. Helmets for touring and town riding are an American innovation now gaining popularity in Europe. The American helmets are made from plastics, and are similar in appearance to motor-cycle helmets. They are not universally popular because many pedal cyclists find they are rather heavy, and in spite of being designed with ventilation holes they are warm to wear.

What are the special features of cycling shoes?

They are lightweight shoes, usually without heels, with thin soles sometimes reinforced by a thin steel plate or wooden insert. Heavier types of touring shoes can be worn for walking short distances, but racing shoes are quite unsuitable for walking in. Most designs have holes in the uppers to keep the feet cool, and are intended for use with shoe plates.

Training and jogging shoes can be satisfactorily used for cycling if they have soles thick enough to cushion the feet from steel pedals. They cannot be fitted with shoe plates.

What is the best type of clothing for wet weather riding?

Experienced cyclists always carry a cape strapped either to the saddle or saddle bag. The cape is the most effective type of protection from rain as it forms an 'umbrella' over the rider's body. It should be large enough to fit over the cycle from the back of the saddle to handlebars. A cape prevents air from circulating round the rider's body, and if overheating is to be avoided it is advisable to shed a layer of clothing. Capes are made in nylon or PVC, and bright fluorescent colours should be chosen as even in daylight motorists' visibility is impaired by heavy rain.

More comfortable and cooler, although offering less protection from the weather, is the racing cape, a long waterproof jacket worn for road racing or training.

Another alternative is a rain suit, comprising over-jacket and trousers. Its main drawback is condensation that forms inside. Over-trousers are too bulky to be entirely satisfactory for cycling wear; an alternative way to protect the legs is with waterproof 'spats' that cover the top of the shoe and extend to just below the knee.

To prevent rain dropping down the back of the neck a sou'wester is the best form of headgear.

8

SAFE CYCLING

What is meant by 'defensive riding'?

At all times, but particularly in traffic, the cyclist should develop the habit of riding defensively. This means thinking ahead and anticipating any potentially dangerous situation so that evasive action can be taken.

Riding defensively means never taking anything for granted where other road users are concerned, and acting decisively so that motorists and pedestrians are in no doubt of your intentions.

It also means careful route planning to avoid the busier roads. It is usually possible to find a safer and more pleasant route through side roads to arrive at the same destination.

Another defensive tactic is to wear at least one light-coloured or fluorescent item of clothing so that you are conspicuous to other road users.

What special problems does the cyclist face in traffic?

Cyclists frequently get into difficulties when turning across the flow of traffic at road junctions and roundabouts. The rider should begin this type of manoeuvre well in advance by looking back to ensure the road is clear. When it is, a signal should be made before moving into position to make the turn.

In practice things do not always go so smoothly. If traffic is too busy, or other road users refuse to acknowledge the cyclist's right of way, discretion is the better part of valour and there is nothing for it but to pull into the left-hand side of the road and wait for the traffic to clear.

Other hazards include parked cars, and when overtaking it is dangerous to weave in and out of parked vehicles. Instead take a smooth line and allow a generous safety margin in case a driver should fling his door open without warning.

When filtering through slow moving traffic, ride slowly and be on the alert for vehicles suddenly turning left or right, pedestrians crossing the road, and vehicles emerging from the left.

When riding in a group should cyclists always remain in single file?

They can ride two abreast but only where road and traffic conditions allow for this to be done in safety without inconveniencing other road users.

Is it possible to receive instruction in bicycle riding?

There are no provisions for teaching adults. The only way to master the art of staying upright on a bicycle is to select a quiet stretch of road and practise by trial and error. However, in the UK children can learn about road safety, practical roadwork and cycle maintenance under the Cycling Proficiency Scheme. The scheme, which is free, is aimed at nine to fourteen year olds. Every year more than 300 000 children take the course, and if they are successful receive a certificate and badge.

Where can I find out more about the Scheme?

Contact your local road safety officer, or write to RoSPA, Cannon House, The Priory, Queensway, Birmingham B4 6BS, Telephone 021-233-2461.

Are any facilities available for cyclists to ride segregated from motor traffic?

Cycleways – networks of roads exclusively for cycles and mopeds – with their own system of underpasses and traffic lights, have been provided in the new towns of Stevenage and Milton Keynes, and are planned for Thamesmead, Middlesborough and Peter-borough. They link people to their work places, schools, shopping or recreation by convenient routes on which hazards are greatly reduced.

Use of the cycleways is not compulsory, and cyclists can use the 'normal' roads if they wish.

Can cyclists ride in bus lanes?

This is allowed by may local authorities. Dual use is indicated by a sign showing a bus and a bicycle.

What is a designated cycle route?

A linked route for cyclists using roads with low traffic volume. It is marked with directional cycle route signs and road signs giving priority to cyclists. This is the most inexpensive means of providing cycling facilities and has been adopted by a number of local authorities.

Are cycleways and cycle routes confined to urban areas?

Bridle paths are open to cyclists, and there are scenic cycle trails such as the Sussex South Downs route or the High Peak trail in Derbyshire.

What are the law's requirements for lighting on cycles?

In the UK a white light must be shown to the front, a red light and reflector to the rear. The reflector and rear light should be on the centre line or off-side of the cycle, not more than 20 in from the rear-most part, and at a height from the ground of between 15 in (38 cm) and 3 ft 6 in (10.7 cm).

Are British Standards applied to cycle lamps?

Rear lamps should conform to BS 3648 and reflectors to BS AU 40LI.

What types of lighting are available?

Two types, battery-powered and dynamo-powered. A typical battery-type front lamp would be powered by a twin-cell 6 V dry battery, and a rear by two single-cell 1.5 V batteries.

Dynamo pulleys are driven from the tyre. The generator can be mounted on the forks, seatstays, or behind the bottom bracket on the chainstays. An exception is the Sturmey-Archer Dyno-hub in which the generator is built into the wheel hub.

Battery front lamps and dynamo headlamps are usually mounted on lamp brackets on the front fork blades. Battery and dynamo rear lights and reflectors are fixed to the off-side seatstay.

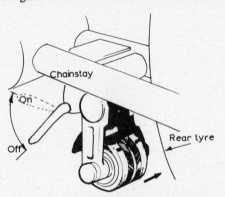

Fig. 40. The Sanyo dynamo pulley, mounted on the chainstays and driven by the rear tyre

What are the advantages and disadvantages of battery and dynamo-powered lamps?

Battery lamps cost less and are marginally lighter in weight. They can easily be fitted or removed from the cycle as required. On the debit side, batteries have a limited life, about three hours of continuous use, and manufacturers still have to perfect a lamp which works satisfactorily without constant attention. Battery lamps have an annoying habit of flickering out without warning, the reason usually being a fault in the switch, contacts or bulb holder.

Dynamo-powered lamps are generally more reliable and give a brighter light. There is of course a certain amount of 'drag' from the generator pulley on the tyre when the lamp is in use, unlike the Dyno-hub in which the 'drag' is constant whether light is needed or not. However, the Dyno-hub is the most trouble-free system of all as its hub generator is well protected from weather and other hazards.

As the dynamo only gives light when the cycle is moving is there a risk of the cyclist breaking the law when he is stationary on the road?

No, the law recognises the problem and it is not illegal to stop with an unlit cycle. Recent innovations in dynamo design have solved the difficulty by incorporating an electronic device that switches the lamps to battery power whenever dynamo revolutions drop below a certain level, thus ensuring a constant light.

What should be checked if the dynamo light goes out?

The most common cause of dynamo light failure is a blown bulb, usually due to vibration. It is advisable to find room in the tool kit for a pair of spare bulbs. Other causes may be loose wires, rusty connections, or a loose earth screw. The screw, usually found on the generator bracket, needs to be screwed well in so that its point goes through the enamel and makes contact with clean bare metal.

What other steps can the cyclist take to make himself more easily visible to other road users?

Extra reflectors can be attached to the backs of the pedals, into the ends of handlebar plugs, and onto spokes, giving side-on reflection.

Reflecting tape can be applied to the rear mudguard, saddlebag, panniers, seatstays and gloves. Mudguards can be light in colour or fluorescent to show up well in the dark.

Reflective surfaces need not be confined to the bicycle. The rider can wear a fluorescent sleeveless tunic, or a fluorescent cross-belt, and can also carry a strap-on battery lamp. Shaped like a torch, it has a double head, showing white to the front and red to the rear, and is strapped to the upper arm.

Is there any device designed to persuade the motorist to give the cyclist more room when overtaking?

A recent innovation is a large circular reflector mounted on the end of a plastics rod. When the rod is fixed to th off-side seat stay it sticks out horizontally about 18 in (460 mm). It has been thoroughly tested and found to be effective in catching the motorist's eye so that he gives the cycle a wider berth.

How should a cyclist indicate the intention to turn?

By making the appropriate hand signal, or by flashing indicators which are mounted on the upper seatstays and are battery-powered. These have only recently been made legal in the UK.

Is it compulsory to fit a bell to a cycle?

The law does not require a cycle to have a bell, although some type of audible warning such as a bell or battery-powered horn is a worthwhile idea. However, in a sudden emergency the cyclist may find he instinctively relies on his own shouted warning rather than a mechanical means.

How can a cycle best be protected against theft?

Buy a sturdy cycle-lock and chain. The most popular type consists of a padlock and a plastics coated chain or cable. Always park the cycle where there are plenty of people about, and chain it to a convenient post, railings or tree. If possible loop the chain through both the frame and wheels – a determined thief will make off with the wheels, leaving the frame behind.

Which accessories are vulnerable to theft?

Front lamps and cycle pumps can easily be slipped off the cycle and should be removed if it is to be left unattended.

What other precautions can be taken?

So that you can give the police a precise description keep a written record of the details of the cycle, including the frame number (usually stamped under the bottom bracket or on the seat lug), details of the components, colour finish and any features such as chromium plating or transfers.

What is the best way to carry shopping on a bicycle?

Never carry a shopping bag on the handlebars. It will pull the steering to one side and may catch in the spokes of the front wheel. A far better solution is a rear carrier mounted over the back wheel. This will carry even quite unwieldy shapes, holding them in place by a spring-loaded clip. The best carriers are made from aluminium alloy, and are fixed to the frame at the brake stirrup bolt and mudguard eyes. Small loads can be carried in a handlebar basket attached to the handlebars. The basket can be either the traditional wicker type, or a wire supermarket type basket.

What are the main types of special cycle bags available?

There are four main types, saddlebags, handlebar bags, front and rear panniers. The most popular is the saddlebag, attached to the saddle by two straps that loop through eyes in the back of the saddle, with a third strap fastened round the seat pillar. The bag is suported by a carrier mounted on the seatstays. A handlebar bag is strapped to the tops of dropped handlebars. A useful feature is a transparent pocket on the top flap, making an ideal place to carry a map so that it can be read without stopping.

The combined capacity of a saddle and handlebar bag should be sufficient for the needs of most people. But the tourist planning a trip lasting several weeks, or who need to carry camping equipment, will also needs pannier bags.

Both types, front and rear panniers, need to be carried on secure carriers fixed over the wheels. The rear carrier can also double as a saddlebag support or be used to carry the cape roll and spare tyre or inner tube.

What are the advantages and disadvantages of the various types of bags?

Although a great deal can be packed into a saddlebag, its main drawback is that it is carried high on the bicycle, making it rather unstable. Handlebar bags are being used more by British cyclists after years of popularity on the Continent. If the bag is strapped directly on to the handlebars, the rider is able only to grip the bottoms of the handlebars or the brake levers. However, this snag has recently been overcome by the introduction of a special clip that holds the bag an inch or so away from the handlebars.

The chief merit of panniers is that they keep the centre of gravity of the bicycle low, which means a more stable and safer ride. Rear panniers need to be mounted well back, otherwise they catch the rider's heels.

What materials are cycle bags made from?

Cotton duck is the traditional material, although this is being superseded by proofed nylon which is just as strong and a good deal lighter.

9

THE SPORT AND PASTIME

What are the main forms of cycle racing practised in Britain?

Road racing, road time trialling, track racing and cyclo-cross.

What is the difference between time trialling and road racing?

Time trials are races against the clock in which the riders start at one minute intervals, and the winner is the one who records the fastest time for the course. In road races the whole field starts together and winner is the first man across the line.

How does track racing differ from road competition?

It takes place on banked oval tracks, with most of the races being of the first-over-the-line variety. Lap distances can be as little as 250 metres and as large as 500 metres. Bankings vary from just a few metres to 50° and track surfaces can be cement, asphalt, or on the best tracks, wood. Grass-track racing is also popular in certain parts of the country, particularly in the North where there are fewer 'hard' tracks than in the South and Midlands. There are indoor tracks in many major cities on the Continent, but in the UK indoor tracks are provided only for short periods to stage a particular event before being dismantled.

What is cyclo-cross?

Cross-country racing on bicycles. Courses usually take in footpaths, cart tracks, a short stretch of road and at least one section where the competitors have to dismount and carry their bicycles on their shoulder. Apart from indoor track racing, cyclo-cross is the only branch of cycle sport to take place during the winter months.

Do women take part in cycle races?

Most races are open for both men and women to compete on equal terms, and there are also races for women only.

Is there an age limit for racing cyclists?

The categories are: juveniles, aged 12 to 16; juniors, aged 16 to 18; seniors, 18 and over; veterans, 40 and over.

How can one take up cycle racing?

By joining a cycling club that is affiliated to the British Cycling Federation. There are more than 1500 affiliated clubs, and to find out about clubs in your region write to the BCF, 70 Brompton Road, London, SW3 1EN. The Federation administers cycle racing in the UK and each year publishes a handbook containing details of all forthcoming road races and track meetings.

Most cycling clubs are also affiliated to the Road Time Trials Council, which is solely responsible for time trialling.

Does the BCF also control cycle speedway?

No, cycle speedway is administered by the Cycle Speedway Council, 9 Meadow Close, Hethersett, Norwich.

Is a reliablility trial a type of race?

No, it is a ride over a set distance for which a standard time is set. Everyone finishing inside the time limit receives a small award such as a certificate. Standards are not too demanding, 100 miles (62 km) in eight hours being a popular trial distance.

How would a frame designed for track racing differ from one intended for road use?

The most noticeable feature is the rear fork ends, they face forwards. Most track races are short, sprint-type events, so comfort is a minor consideration in frame design. Fork rake is steep, making for a short wheelbase. Clearances under the front crown and rear seatstay bridge are kept to a minimum, and chain and seatstays are made from heavy gauge tubing, all to ensure that the frame is as responsive and rigid as possible when subjected to the track sprinter's explosive effort. Track frames are designed with high bottom brackets, giving about 11 in (300 mm) pedal clearance on banked tracks.

The road racer stays in the saddle for hours on end, and needs a frame that will give a comfortable ride, with shallower angles and a longer wheelbase, making it both manouevreable and capable of absorbing some road vibration.

What is 'slipstreaming'?

If two cyclists ride in single file the second can travel at exactly the same speed as the first without expending nearly as much energy. If the front wheel is kept as close as possible to the leader's rear wheel the second rider is sheltered from the wind resistance that becomes an increasingly important factor as the cyclist's speed increases.

For this reason a group of riders can maintain a much higher speed than a solo cyclist by frequent change of leader.

Is a standard sports machine suitable for racing?

A good quality lightweight model bought 'off the peg' from a cycle shop can be raced in road events without modification if its specification includes such items as an alloy chainset, tubular tyres and derailleur gears, equipment favoured by most competitors in road races and time trials. The new narrow section 27 × 1 in wired-on tyres are an excellent substitute for expensive tubulars, particularly in time trials.

What are the differences between components on road and track machines?

The road racing machine is equipped with 5, 10 or 12 gears, two brakes, quick-release hubs, a bottle, a pump and a spare tubular tyre. Track cycles are stripped down to the bare essentials. Instead of derailleur gears there is a single fixed wheel, which is also used for slowing the cycle as there are no brakes. Wheel hubs are secured by track nuts, rather than a quick-release mechanism which could be a safety hazard in a crash. The handlebars and handlebar stem are steel rather than aluminium alloy. Tubulars are very light, 4 to 6 oz as against 8 to 10 oz for road racing. Large flange hubs are preferred to small flange as the wheels need to be as strong as possible to withstand the stresses imposed by the bankings.

What are the special features of a cyclo-cross machine?

Low gear ratios, to allow the rider to pedal through mud and up steep climbs. Heavy tyres weighing about 18 oz, with a studded tread. Cantilever-type brakes for maximum clearances between tyres and fork crown and seatstay bridge where the wheel could easily become clogged with leaves and mud.

Are there organisations that cater for the cyclist who is interested in touring rather than racing?

Most cyclists in the UK find it worthwhile to be a member of the national touring body, the Cyclist's Touring Club, if only for the third party insurance cover and free legal aid that it provides. The CTC's services to members also include advice on touring routes and technical matters. The Club annually publishes a handbook which lists recommended accommodation and repairers, and also produces a bimonthly magazine, *Cycletouring*.

There are more than 200 'District Associations', local sections of the CTC which organise a full programme of touring activities, such as Sunday runs or youth hostelling weekends.

The CTC frequently represents the interests of cyclists on public bodies and when legislation affecting cycling is being considered. The CTC address is Cotterell House, Godalming, Surrey.

Do other countries have equivalent national bodies to the BCF and CTC?

Yes, here is a list of some of the overseas cycling organisations.

Canada – Canadian Cycling Association, 333 River Road, Vanier, Ottawa, Ontario, K11 8B9. Caters for all aspects of cycling in Canada.

France – Federation Française de Cyclisme, 43 rue de Dunkerque, 75ᵉ Paris. Controls cycle racing in France.
Federation Française de Cyclotourisme, 8 rue Jean-Marie Jego, 75ᵉ13 Paris. The national organisation for cycle touring.

Ireland – Irish Cycling Federation, 287 Castledown, Leixlip, co. Kildare. Promotes all facets of cycling.

Netherlands – Koninklijke Nederlandsche Toeristenbond. Wassenaarsweg 220, The Hague. Provides information on cycle routes and cycle tours in Holland, and arranges cycling package holidays.

USA – League of American Wheelmen, PO Box 988, Baltimore, Maryland 21203. A touring organisation with more than 400 member clubs. Arranges rallies and tours, advises on touring, insurance and legal matters.

What are the main features of a cycle built for touring?

There are only minor differences between racing and touring cycles. The touring machine has deeper fork clearance to accommodate mudguards, and will have at least one carrier to support a saddlebag or panniers. Tyres will be medium or heavyweight high pressures, and there will be at least 36 spokes in each wheel, perhaps 40 in the rear if the cycle is to be heavily laden for a long tour. The main difference between the two types of machine lies in the gear ratios. The tourist needs to carry spare clothing, tools and so on with him, and will gear down accordingly. Low gears are also a necessity in many popular touring areas where there are plenty of hills, such as the Lake District, North Wales or the West Country.

Are cycles still carried free on railways?

Carriage of cycles is free on most services. The only limitations are on some of the high speed train routes, where because of the train design luggage space is limited and on rush-hour commuter trains into major cities. Cycles being carried by rail should be placed in the guard's van with a label attached showing the owner's name, address and stations of departure and arrival.

The alternative is to carry the machine as a piece of luggage. Folding cycles pack away into their own nylon bag, and 'transit bags' are also available to carry conventional cycles with the wheels removed.

Which is the best way to carry a cycle by car?

It can be mounted upside down on a roof rack and secured by straps (toe-straps are ideal) at the handlebars and saddle. Kits are available for adapting roof racks to carry cycles, and there are custom-made cycle racks for fitting either on to the roof or to the back of the car.

Is it possible to take a cycle by air?

Airlines will accept bicycles that have been partially dismantled to make a more manageable shape. Wheels can be removed and strapped both sides of the frame, handlebars turned sideways and strapped to the top tube, and pedals removed.

10

MAINTENANCE AND REPAIRS

What items are required to make up a basic tool-kit?

The following tools should be sufficient for most minor repair and maintenance jobs: a multi-purpose or dumbbell-type spanner, screwdriver, pliers, light hammer, puncture repair kit and three tyre levers. If more ambitious repair and maintenance jobs are to be attempted, such as replacing and adjusting hub or bottom bracket bearings, or replacing main components, a comprehensive set of spanners will be needed (including both metric and Imperial sizes). Open-ended spanners are the best for most purposes, with a $\frac{3}{8} \times \frac{5}{16}$ ring spanner recommended for wheel hub nuts.

A good quality lightweight machine will need specialist tools, including a chainwheel extractor, for fitting and removing alloy cotterless chainsets; allen keys to fit socket screws on handlebar stems, seat lugs and chainrings; a rivet extractor for $\frac{3}{32}$ in chains; two thin-section cone spanners for adjusting hub bearings; a soft metal punch for bottom bracket lockrings; a freewheel remover and a spoke nipple key.

Which parts of a cycle need oiling and greasing?

All the moving parts such as hubs, pedals and gears require regular lubrication. Particular attention should be paid to the brake stirrups and cables and headset bearings.

What are the best types of lubricant?

A light cycle oil applied from an oil can with a fine nozzle is the best lubricant for bearings and cable. A spray-on aerosol lubricant is recommended for the chain and gears as it is non-greasy and repels water. When replacing hub, bottom bracket, headset and pedal bearings pack them in light grease.

How frequently should lubrication be carried out?

Under normal conditions about once every two weeks. More frequently if the cycle has been in constant use or ridden in wet conditions.

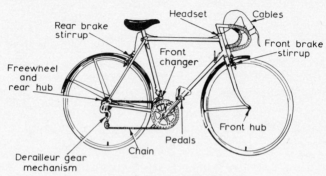

Fig. 41. Lubrication points

How should oil be applied to the brakes?

Coat both the nipple and plain ends of the cable with a film of oil. Pull the brake on and off several times so that the oil works its way along the cable into the outer casing (the same applies to gear cables). Also apply oil to the pivot bolts and springs on the stirrup, taking care to avoid oil getting onto the brake blocks.

How are headset bearings oiled?

Place the cycle upside down, and the ball bearings should just be visible in the top and bottom head races. The oil can be applied direct.

Which components have lubrication points?

Oil holes are sometimes provided on the barrels of the hubs, bottom bracket shell and pedal dust caps.

What other uses do oil and grease have in cycle maintenance?

When fitting the saddle pillar and handlebar stems, coat the parts to be inserted into the frame with a small amount of grease for easier fitting and protection against corrosion. A drop of oil should be applied to threads before fitting such components as pedals.

What is the best position for the cycle when it is being worked on?

It can be placed upside down, if care is taken to protect the saddle and handlebars. This is not ideal, and professionals use special stands that hold the cycle about hand high. However, stands are expensive, and a cheap alternative is to hang the cycle from a shed or garage roof, using string or chain at the saddle and handlebars.

How can wheels be removed without the tyres dislodging the brake blocks?

If the brakes have a quick-release device on the stirrup or lever, release it to open the stirrup out. Alternatively, unfasten the cable clamp nut to free the cable, or remove one of the brake shoes.

Which freewheel sprocket should the chain be on when the back wheel is removed?

The gear lever should be pushed forward into top gear so that the chain is on the smallest sprocket. To keep the chain out of the way while the wheel is out, tie the chain to the rear brake bridge. Keep the chain on the small sprocket when replacing the wheel.

What are the snags to look for when fitting wheels into the frame?

The wheels must be central in the frame otherwise steering will be affected. Particular case should be taken when fitting the rear wheel as there is a good deal of adjustment in the rear fork ends. It is important that wheel nuts or quick-release mechanisms are securely tightened. A loose wheel will pull over in the frame as soon as any pressure is applied on the pedals.

What items are needed to repair a puncture?

The basic items in a repair kit are adhesive patches, a tube of rubber solution and fine sandpaper. Also useful would be French chalk, a canvas tyre patch and an indelible pencil.

How can the puncture be located?

If the hole is not large enough to be easily spotted, immerse the tube in water until a stream of bubbles reveals the puncture. Mark the spot with indelible pencil.

How is the puncture repaired?

Clean the area around the hole with sandpaper; this will also roughen the tube to aid adhesion of the patch. Following the instructions on the repair kit, select a patch large enough to well cover the hole, and spread the solution thinly on the tube. Most rubber solutions are best left until almost dry before the patch is applied. After fitting the patch dust the area with french chalk to prevent the tube sticking to the outer cover.

Before re-fitting the tyre examine it closely to find what caused the puncture. A flint or thorn may still be sticking through, ready to puncture the tube again. Another possible cause is a rim tape that may have shifted, exposing a sharp spoke end.

How should a puncture in a tubular tyre be dealt with?

There is no question of carrying out a road-side repair. The inner tube is sealed inside the tyre which is sewn up at the base. A spare tyre should always be carried for such emergencies. The punctured tyre can be taken off and a spare fitted in a couple of minutes.

Puncture repairing is a tricky job and there are specialist repairers of tubulars who will do the job for you. But if you prefer to save expense and do it yourself, you can buy a repair kit which in addition to solution and patches includes a needle, thimble and strong thread.

How can the puncture be located?

By inflating the tyre and immersing it in water. Ignore the bubbles that will come streaming from the base of the valve – this is simply air escaping from between the tube and outer cover – and instead look for bubbles coming from a hole in the tread or sidewalls.

How is the tyre opened to gain access to the punctured tube?

Pull about 5 in (125 mm) of base tape away from the area of the puncture. This will reveal the stitches which should be cut away with a sharp blade, cutting upwards to avoid nicking the tube which is just underneath.

Take a few inches of tube out and inflate slightly so that escaping air reveals the position of the hole. Repair in the normal way, using the extra-thin patches supplied with the kit. Check the inside of the tyre for whatever may have caused the puncture, and sew up the tyre again using the original needle holes. Finally, stick the base tape back into place and inflate the tyre.

INDEX

QUESTIONS & ANSWERS

PAINTING AND DECORATING

A Fulcher and others

The authors, with many years' practical and teaching experience, provide a wealth of information on the materials, processes and methods of working required for decorating a house both inside and outside. The book will answer many DIY questions and also be a reference source for craft students.

CONTENTS: Tools and equipment. Preparation and painting of surfaces. Wallcoverings. Paint defects. Scaffolding. Work procedure. Index.

128 pages   0 408 00321 9

Newnes Technical Books
Borough Green, Sevenoaks, Kent TN15 8PH

CARPENTRY AND JOINERY

A R WHITTICK

The basic aspects of the work of the carpenter and joiner are explained in a way that will appeal both to the handyman who wants to know how to maintain the joinery and timber structure of his home, and to the craft student.

CONTENTS: Hand and portable power tools. Timber and built-up materials. Timber defects, pests and diseases. Joints, fastenings and fixings. Temporary work. Carcassing. First and second fixing. Ironmongery and fittings. Basic woodworking machinery. Joinery. Preserving and finishing timber. Fences and gates. Repairs and maintenance. Index.

160 pages   0 408 00375 8

Newnes Technical Books
Borough Green, Sevenoaks, Kent TN15 8PH

Questions & Answers

QUESTIONS & ANSWERS

CENTRAL HEATING

W H JOHNSON

This is a brief but comprehensive survey of domestic heating systems for both layman and student. The emphasis throughout is on fuel (and hence cost) saving, and how to achieve an acceptable standard of comfort for the least expenditure of energy.

CONTENTS: Insulation. Central heating systems. Wet systems. Boilers. Dry systems. The fuels. Domestic hot water. Controls. Some useful calculations. Some conclusions. Index.

128 pages   0 408 00459 2

ewnes Technical Books
Borough Green, Sevenoaks, Kent TN15 8PH

Questions and Answers

PLUMBING

A Johnson

This book gives concise and reliable information on the principles of good plumbing design and on the use of plumbing materials both old and new. Guidance on calculations is included, and there is useful tabulated information.

CONTENTS: Pipes and pipework. Water supply. Sanitary appliances. Drainage. Above ground drainage. Domestic hot water supply. Sheet weathering. Calculations. Appendix. Index.

96 pages   0 408 00136 4

Newnes Technical Books
Borough Green, Sevenoaks, Kent TN15 8PH